RWANDAN

GENOCIDE

The Unspeakable Evils of Ethnic Cleansing and Genocide in Rwanda

Dr. Julia Sanders

Table of Contents

The Rwandan Genocide

There are few crimes more heinous than murder, ending an innocent human life is an unforgivable act that's consequences cannot be taken back. And yet, there are occasions where murder is taken to a new extreme in the form of genocide. In 1948, a group called The United Nations Genocide Convention was founded and as the experts on genocide, they define it as "acts committed with intent to destroy, in whole or in part, a national, ethnic, racial or religious group."

With how far humanity has come as a whole, it's easy to think that something as terribly monstrous as the intentional targeting of a single group of people for mass murder with the hope of total extinction would be something the world hasn't seen in centuries. Unfortunately, that isn't true.

One such group to suffer an event to fit that definition was the Tutsi people in Rwanda. They were targeted during a period that lasted 100 days in 1994 by members of the majority government of Hutu and it is estimated that 500,000 to 1,000,000 Rwandan lives were taken. The genocide began on April 7th and lasted until July 15th. The Tutsi lost as much s 70% of its population and the Pygmy Batwa suffered the loss of 30% of their population as well.

Tutsi is the colloquial and most commonly used term for the Rwandan social class of people that was considered the highest, which came from their original name Abatutsi, though they are also called the

Watutsi, Wahima, Wahuma, Imfure, and Wahinda. They are located within the African Great Lakes region and their rank in social class allowed them extra privileges within their homeland and beyond by feudal law.

Their genocide was plotted out by people involved with the core political elite, which included many national government officials that held top positions. Those that carried out the genocide itself were soldiers of the Rwandan army, government-supported militias, and the Gendarmerie. Two of the militias were the Impuzamugambi and the Interahamwe.

The background context behind this genocide was the Rwandan Civil War, which began in 1990. It was an ongoing conflict between the government (which was run by Hutu) and the Rwandan Patriotic Front (which was largely consistent of Tutsi refugees). The Tutsi in the Rwandan Patriotic Front were refugees of the Hutu revolt against colonial rule in 1959 and had fled to Uganda for safety. The Rwandan's gained independence in 1962, but the Rwandan Patriotic Front continued to face violent attacks. A ceasefire finally settled in 1963 after the Hutu government of Juvénal Habyarimana was put under international pressure. The birth of the Arusha Accords followed, which was meant to feed the peace by sharing power with the government and the Rwandan Patriotic Front.

Unfortunately, there were many conservative Hutu that were against this agreement because they felt that it conceded to the demands of the enemy. The Akazu were among these opposing Hutu. An ideology known as the Hutu Power came about, portraying the Rwandan Patriotic Front as a foreign power that was made up of non-Christian people that were intent on bringing power back to the Tutsi monarchy and forcing Hutus into slavery. This prospect made many Hutus react with extreme opposition. It is worth noting that machete imports rose in Rwanda during the lead-up to the genocide.

Burundian President Cyprien Ntaryamira and Habyarimana were on a plane flying above Habyarimana's home on April 6th of 1994 when they were shot down as a means of the assassination while they were on their descent into Kigali. There was one person that survived the crash, but they died before they reached the hospital. When Habyarimana died, so did the peace accords.

It was as soon as the following day that the genocidal killings began. Militia, police, and soldiers started with key members of the Tutsi, political leaders that might be able to seize control while the government was weak, and moderate Hutu military that got in the way. To aid in finding and eradicating all of the Tutsi, there were roadblocks and checkpoints erected where anyone coming through had to show their national ID card of Rwanda, which had included ethnic information and classification since 1933 when the concept was introduced by the Belgian colonial government.

The groups that came together in order to enact this genocide also put pressure on regular citizens to arm themselves against their Tutsi neighbors with deadly weapons. These messages went as far as to encourage Hutu civilians to main, rape, and kill these people. If they weren't intending on stealing their property, they were to destroy it so that no other Tutsi could reclaim it.

In retaliation, the Rwandan Patriotic Front took on the offensive again and began rapidly taking control of the country in the north and then in mid-July they took Kigali, which was what ended the genocide.

Many names in world power were criticized both during and after these events. the United Nations, the United Kingdom, the United States, and Belgium were among these names for their lack of action and the weakness of their force and mandate of the

UN Assistance Mission for Rwanda peacekeepers. France was also criticized for allegedly supporting the Hutu government after the genocidal killings had started.

There was a profound and lasting impact left on Rwanda and their neighboring countries by the Rwandan Genocide. Because rape was pervasively used as a weapon of war, there was a dramatic increase in HIV infections and HIV infected babies were born to women that had just been infected themselves. Many houses were run by widows and orphan children. The country's economy was crippled by the sudden and severe depopulation as well,

Because the Rwandan Patriotic Front's victory meant they had a strong military and the government was now in their full control, many Hutu fled to the countries around Rwanda. Many of them ended up in the eastern portion of what was then called Zaire, and is now known as the Democratic Republic of Congo. These people were known as the Hutu genocidaires, and they started to group together again along the borders of Rwanda in refugee camps. The Rwandan Patriotic Front led the government, which declared this regrouping as a reason to fear further genocide attempts, so they invaded Zaire through military incursions that like the First and Second Congo Wars that were meant to disband the threat.

The impetus for the creation of the International Criminal Court was this genocide, and it was created in order to replace ad hoc tribunals for the prosecution of genocide, war crimes, and crimes against humanity.

There are two public holidays in Rwanda that mourn the genocide. The national mourning period begins with the national commemoration of Kwibuka on April 7th and ends on July 4th with the Liberation Day. The whole week after the 7th of April is known as Icyunamo and is an official week long period of mourning.

To this day, the armed struggled between the Rwanda Hutu and Tutsi continue, with people from both groups still living throughout the region in refugee camps.

The History of Rwanda

The first group of people to inhabit Rwanda
was known as the Twa, and they are an
aboriginal group of pygmy hunter-gatherers
that still remain there today. They first
settled in between 8000 BC and 3000 BC.
There were also a number of Bantu groups
that cleared forested land so that they could
gather the wood and make space for houses
and farmlands between 700 BC and 1500 AD
after migrating into Rwanda. Within these
Bantu groups were the Hutu and the Tutsi,
and there are two big theories regarding
their migrations. One is that the Hutu came
first and the Tutsi followed afterward,
distinctly remaining their own group and
forming a distinct racial group. The other big
theory is that both the Hutu and the Tutsi

came in slow migration, showing up in small groups from neighboring regions and then integrating into society instead of remaining separate. In the latter theory, there would have been no distinction between the Hutu and the Tutsi until later. It would also mean that the distinction was not racial, but based on caste or class based on the fact that the Hutu farmed the land while the Tutsi herded cattle. All three of these original, native groups of Rwanda speak the same language and are known together as the Banyarwanda.

The people coalesced, with the first instance being clans known as ubwoko and the second coming by 1700 in the form of eight kingdoms. The Tutsi Nyiginya clan ruled the Kingdom of Rwanda and stepped up their dominance in the mid-eighteenth century.

They expanded their territory by conquests and assimilation, growing to their biggest under the reign of King Kigeli Rwabugiri. During his reign, the kingdom expanded to the west and north. He also began a number of administrative reforms, including the ubuhake, which had Tutsi citizens gave their cattle, and therefore status and privilege, to the Hutu or Tutsi that needed them in exchange for personal and economic services. Another administrative reform was called the uburetwa and it forced Hutu to work beneath Tutsi chiefs. The changes made by Rwabugiri deepened the division of power and the socio-economic differences between the Tutsi and the Hutu.

In 1884, The Berlin Conference gave the land to Germany, whose policy then included ruling by proxy through the Rwandan monarchy. An additional event caused because of this system was the beginning of small European troop numbers colonizing. The belief of these European colonists was that the Tutsi had migrated from Ethiopia, which made them more Caucasian than the Hutu. This belief led them to view the Tutsi as racially superior, which meant they were also seen as better candidates for colonial administrative tasks. This was beneficial to Tutsi rule because it gave them Germans, which King Yuki V Musings used to add strength to his rule.

Again, Rwanda was passed on to another leading nation in 1919, which came to being after Belgian forces invaded and took Burundi and Rwanda during World War I. A League of Nations mandate gave Belgium formal control. At first, the German's system of controlling the government through the monarchy continued but began a more direct colonial rule policy in 1926 that was much like the style of ruling used in the Belgian Congo. The uburetwa that put the Hutu beneath the Tutsi was extended and strengthened, and the chieftaincy was simplified by making it smaller and focusing even further on giving all local power to the Tutsi. They also oversaw the Tutsi chiefs through a land reform process that seized grazing areas that had belonged to Hutu collectives up until then privatized the lands, giving back very little compensation. Modernization came after Belgians brought large-scale advancements in health, education, agricultural supervision, and public works in the 1930s. Even through the modernization, the Tutsi social supremacy was solidly in place, which disenfranchised the Hutu and forced them into large labor projects. Up until 1935, it was possible for Hutu to pass as honorary Tutsi, but the introduction of new identity cards that labeled citizens and outed them as Twa, Hutu, or Tutsi made it impossible for any Hutu to become as privileged as any Tutsi. Their social class was written right on the card that identified them legally and was therefore impossible to hide. The Belgians also brought the Catholic Church with them, because the information given to them by the local clergy was an asset to them. It became a means of social advancement to convert, so many people in Rwanda became Catholic.

The spirit of freedom and independence that came after World War II was not felt in Rwanda, and instead, the citizens were full of resentment based on inter-war social reforms that (coupled with sympathy from the Catholic Church for the Hutu) birthed an emancipation movement. It became clear to the Catholic missionaries that at least one of the reasons that the Hutu were so underprivileged was due to their decisions to continuously empower the Tutsi elite, which led them to promote a sizeable amount of Hutu to educated elite and clergy positions, which provided a bit of balance to the previous political order. However, the monarchy and more powerful Tutsi could tell that the Hutu were gaining influence and fearing a loss of Tutsi control and privilege, they demanded independence immediately, on their own terms.

The first documentation that officially labeled the Tutsi and the Hutu different races was the Bahuto Manifesto, which was written in 1957 by a group of Hutu scholars. This document also made a demand based on statistical law for the power to further transfer from the Tutsi to the Hutu.

A Hutu sub-chief by the name of Dominique Mbonyumutwa was attacked on November 1st of 1959 by pro-Tutsi party supporters in Kigali. Though Mbonyumutwa did survive the attack, there were rumors spread that said he had been killed, which enraged Hutu activists. Their response was to look for blood, and they began the Rwandan Revolution by killing Tutsi. The deaths included ordinary citizens as well as the elite. The Tutsi responded in kind, marking Rwandan soil with attacks of their own. Unfortunately for the Tutsi, the Belgian administration had already given the Hutu their full support and they were ready to change the Tutsi domination. By the early 1960s, Hutu people replaced most of the Tutsi chiefs, by Belgian order. Mid-year commune elections were organized by the Belgians as well, which brought the Hutu majority in overwhelming numbers. The Tutsi King was officially deposed and the country gained its independence in 1962 with the creation of a Hutu dominated republic.

With the Hutu purging the land of Tutsi citizens during the revolution, Tutsi fled the country in exile and settled in Uganda, Zaire, Burundi, and Tanzania. These four countries are neighbors to Rwanda, and are the closest places to go for safety but were also the host countries for many of the Tutsi ancestors. They were considered refugees, even when returning to the places their families originated. That added to their desire to make their return to Rwanda. They gathered and armed themselves, returning to Rwanda in groups that were called inyenzi to launch attacks that were mostly unsuccessful. These attacks led to more Tutsi exiles and murders. There were more than 300,000 Tutsi exiles that had been forced to flee by 1964, an exile they would be forced to continue to live for three decades.

The discrimination that had led to Tutsi domination had come full circle and now favored the Hutu instead. The heavily one-sided favoring of the Hutu continued in Rwanda itself, though the amount of violence against the Tutsi did lower after the coup in 1973 that put President Juvenal Habyarmana into power.

500 refugees that had grouped together in Uganda in the 1980s fought against the rebel National Resistance Army, led by Fred Rwigyema, in the Ugandan Bush War. This put Yoweri Museveni in power after he overthrew Milton Obote. The soldiers that fought against the National Resistance Army stayed in the Ugandan army after Museveni was inaugurated as the Ugandan president while also secretly planning an invasion through a covert network against Rwanda.

Rwigyema led another force, this time his troops numbered at over 4,000 rebels from Uganda, and they marched under the Rwandan Patriotic Front's banner as they invaded Rwanda. Rwigyema himself only made it three days before he was killed, and it became increasingly obvious that they would not be able to continue fighting when

Zaire and France showed their support of the Rwandan army by sending forces to help them fight against the Tutsi and stop the invasion. The soldier to take command of the now leader-less Tutsi forces was Rwigyema's deputy, a man by the name of Paul Kagame. He organized a tactical retreat that led them to an area in northern Rwanda called the Virunga Mountains through Uganda. Once they reached their final destination, he was able to get more weapons and organize the army while recruiting and organizing fundraising with the Tutsi diaspora.

The war was brought back to life when Paul Kagame restarted it in January of 1991 by taking the town of Ruherengeri in northern Rwanda by surprise. The surprise attack resulted in a capture of the town for the Rwandan Patriotic Front that they were able to hold for a day before making a retreat into the forests. This course of action continued for a full year, with the Rwandan Patriotic Front taking control of border towns for periods of time with a hit-and-run style of guerrilla warfare, but they weren't able to make any real significant progress against the Rwandan army.

After a multiparty coalition style government formed in Kigali in June of 1992, the Rwandan Patriotic Front officially announced their intention to ceasefire. They then moved to Arusha, Tanzania to meet with the Rwandan government to begin negotiations. Less than a year later in the early months of 1992, campaigns began between several Hutu extremist groups that brought on large amounts of violence against the Tutsi. Peace talks were suspended on the

Rwandan Patriotic Front's side in response, and they launched another major attack against the Hutu in Rwanda. This earned them a large piece of land that spanned across the northern part of the country. They could have left it there and continued to face war-like intentions from both Hutu and Tutsi, but peace negations were eventually resumed and took place in Arusha again. The result was a list of agreements that were called the Arusha Accords, and they were signed officially in August of 1993. The Arusha Accords put the Rwandan Patriotic Front in what they called a Broad-Based Transitional Government as well as within the ranks of the national army. Now that the violence was announced to be over, the peacekeeping force known as the United Nations Assistance Mission for Rwanda arrived in Kigali to oversee the Rwandan Patriotic Front move into the national parliament building in their own base, which was to be theirs while the Broad-Based Transitional Government was set up.

Statistically speaking, the amount of violence against the Tutsi was lower and the economy saw a greater prosperity under the early ruling years of Habyarimana's regime. However, there were still many figures in the country that were very anti-Tutsi. One of these was the first lady Agathe Habyarimana and her family, who were known as the clan de Madame and members of the akazu. President Habyarimana was heavily reliant on their support to keep up his regime. They were able to exploit the Hutu population's fear of the Tutsi after the Rwandan Patriotic Front invaded the country in 1990. This exploitation pushed forward anti-Tutsi actions that were called Hutu Power. From there, government members and military officers created a magazine that would become popular across the country they called Kangura. Within this magazine, anti-Tutsi propaganda was regularly published, including a set of explicit racist guidelines called the Hutu Ten Commandments that called any Hutu that dared to marry a Tutsi a traitor. The Coalition for the Defense of the Republic party was created by anti-Tutsi hardliners in 1992, which had affiliations with the ruling party, though they were much more right wing and were critical of what they saw as softness towards the Rwandan Patriotic Front from the president.

After the ceasefire agreement that was made in 1992, many of the Hutu extremists within the national army and the government became worried that the Tutsi would be included in the government and began actively making plots against the president. There were attempts made to remove the extremists and hardliners from their senior positions in the army by Habyarimana, but he wasn't able to get them all out. Theoneste Bagosora and Augustin Ndlindiliyimana were akuza affiliates that both managed to keep their powerful positions, which allowed the hardline families to maintain their connection with power. There were campaigns of localized Tutsi murders throughout all of 1992, carried out by hardliners. These campaigns culminated in January of 1993 with local Hutu and extremists having killed an estimated 300 people. These 300 murders were announced as the official primary motive when the Rwandan Patriotic Front replied with its own hostile actions in February of 1993. The only effect these hostile actions had was to strengthen the support people had for the Hutu extremists.

In the middle of 1993, the political stage was split into three, with the Habyarimana government, the Hutu Power movement, and the traditional moderate opposition sharing the roles of major forces. Only the CDR was exclusively loyal to just one side, all other parties were split into groups that were in support of the Hutu Power movement and those that were in the moderate opposition group. To make things even more confusion, there were members of both groups claiming to be the official leaders of their party. Even members of the ruling party belonged to a wing in support of the Hutu Power movement, and they were all unhappy with Habyarimana's decision to sign a deal for peace. Militia groups composed of radical youths were born, falling to the Hutu Power movement's side. One of these militia groups was called the Interahamwe, and they were affiliated with the ruling party. Another was the Impuzamugambi, which belonged to the CDR. The national army trained these militias, and sometimes the French would help in this training. Unknown to the French, these militias would then take their training and use it to move across the country and slaughter people in massacres.

The Prelude to Mass Murder

There are various theories within the historical community around the specific date that the proposal to kill every Tutsi that was in Rwanda was made as their final solution. One historian says that the official date was in 1990 after the Rwandan Patriotic Front invaded for the first time. Another historian says that the official date was in 1992 after Habyarimana started to negotiate with the Rwandan Patriotic Front. Potentially coincidentally, the Rwandan government started handing out weaponry to their citizens and training them so that they'd be able to use them in combat. Officially, these actions were made in the name of civil defense against the Rwandan Patriotic Front threat. These weapons, like machetes, were later used in the genocide. A large number of munitions and grenades were also purchased by Rwanda in the late months of 1990. During this time, the Rwandan army grew exponentially at a rapid rate. They had been less than 10,000 troops strong, but in just one year their numbers reached 30,000. The only apparent downside to the speed in which the army's numbers grew was the obvious divide between the elite Presidential Guard and Gendarmerie units, both of which were already battle ready and well trained, and the ordinary file and rank of the new recruits, that were poorly disciplined in comparison.

Regardless of when the decision to move towards genocide was first proposed, the Hutu Power movement started to put together a list of people they dubbed traitors and were planning to kill in March of 1993. It is very likely that Habyarimana's name was also written somewhere on these lists, based on the CDR's very public accusations against him of treason. Radio Rwanda, the national radio station, was also accused of becoming too liberal and it was said that they supported the opposition. So the Hutu Power movement created their own radio station and called it Radio Télévision Libre des Mille Collines. Not surprisingly, this radio station's programming broadcast obscene jokes and music as well as racist propaganda. It also became very popular across the country. Studies that were taken later attribute at least 10% of the general violence that happened during the Rwandan genocide to the programs on this radio station. In 1993, the import numbers for machetes and other tools that could be used as weaponry skyrocketed, reaching a number far higher than any possibly agricultural needs. These tools included items like saws, scissors, and razor blades and were distributed by the hardliner families.

Melchior Ndadaye was elected in June of 1993 as Burundi's first ever Hutu president, and he was then assassinated in October of the same year by extremist Tutsi army officers. This act of violence caused a dramatic response from citizens and strengthened the Hutu idea that the Tutsi could not be trusted because they were enemies. There could not be a more advantageous situation for the Hutu Power movements and the CDR to take advantage of, and when they realized it, the idea of a final solution that would wipe the Tutsi out completely was put at the top of their agenda. The plans officially began and those responsible for organizing it were certain that they would be able to convince the Hutu population to help them carry out this genocide after they saw how angry the public was after Ndadaye was murdered. After their origins as a subservient group, the Hutu were also predisposed to being obedient to the orders of authority. To help raise the death rate as quickly and efficiently as possible, the leaders within the Hutu Power movement gave the Interahamwe and other militia groups high-powered weaponry like AK-47s, which was a large upgrade to their previous arsenal of machetes and other hand-held weapons.

On October 5th of 1993, the Resolution 872 established the UNAMIR force, which had the consent of both parties that were involved in the civil war.

A commander of UNAMIR by the name of General Romeo Dallaire sent a fax to the UN Headquarters on the 11th of January in 1994. This fax said that he had a high level informant that had given him information in regards to plans within the Hutu militia to distribute weaponry through their ranks so that they could kill Belgian members in UNAMIR, with the hope of forcing Belgium to withdraw. The informant was a local politician and he had been ordered to make all of the Tutsi in Kigali register and came up with an estimation that they could kill 1,000 Tutsi people in twenty minutes until all of the Tutsis were exterminated. The informant and his family requested protection through Dallaire, though Kofi Annan forbade it repeatedly, waiting until after he was given guidance from headquarters. He continued to forbid it, even after the genocide had already begun, even though he had the authority to approve it. He stated that he had not done so under the Article 2(4) of the Charter, although the technicalities of the situation state that it would have been an intervention hosted by the UN itself and not someone who was a member of state. Because there was authorization from the UN Security Council and both parties had agreed to have UNIMAR step in and assist, it is argued that they could not have been charged with intervening.

The Rwandan President Juvénal Habyarimana and the Hutu president of Burundi Cyprien Ntaryamira were preparing to land in Kigali on April 6th in 1994 when they were shot down in an attack that killed everyone on the plane. Though an investigation hosted later by the Rwandan government put the blame on Hutu extremists and the same culprit seemed to be blamed again in 2012 by a French investigation, both the Hutu and the Tutsi were disputed as the party responsible for the assassinations of the two Hutu presidents. Though there are many arguments about who it was that fired the missile that brought down the plane, there isn't much to argue about when it is said that this assassination was the catalyst that allowed for the following genocide.

A crisis committee was created the same evening after Habyarimana died, with members like Colonel Theoneste Bagosora, Major General Augustin Ndindiliyimana, and a number of other senior officers on the army staff. Bagosora was the leader of this group, though Ndindiliyimana was a more senior officer. The next in line in the legal line of succession was the Prime Minister, Agathe Uwilingiyimana, but her authority wasn't recognized by the committee, despite Dallaire meeting with the committee that night in order to insist she be put in charge. Uwilingiyimana opposed this idea and accused her of being unable to shoulder the tough responsibility of governing the nation. Bagosora insisted that the committee had justifiable cause to exist because they needed to avoid any uncertainty in the government after their president had died. He also worked to convince the Rwandan Patriotic Front and UNIMAR that their existence was calming the Presidential Guard, who he accused of being out of control without an obvious leader to their government. He assured both the Rwandan Patriotic Front and UNIMAR that they would continue to follow the Arusha agreement.

Ten Belgian soldiers were sent by UNAMIR to transport Prime Minister Uwilingiyimana to the Radio Rwanda offices to speak with the nation. They had to cancel their plan when the Presidential Guard invaded and took control of the radio station, refusing to allow Uwilingiyimana the opportunity to speak on air. A group of soldiers and a number of civilians took an opportunity later in the morning to overwhelm the guards that were protecting Uwilingiyimana and forced them to give up their weapons. The ten Belgian soldiers were then brought to the Camp Kigali military base, tortured, and killed. Both Uwilingiyimana and her husband were murdered that morning, though fortunately, their children were able to hide behind furniture and hide until they were rescued later by the Senegalese UNIMAR officer by the name of Mbaye Diagne. The commanding officer of the unit of the Presidential Guard that was responsible for carrying out these murders was tried by a court in Belgium in 2017 and sentenced to twenty years of imprisonment.

On top of the assassination of Uwilingiyimana, the extremists responsible spent the night of April 6th and the morning of April 7th following a list with the names of prominent moderate journalists and politicians with the intention of killing them all. Some of those that were killed that night include Minister of Agriculture Frederic Nzamurambaho, President of the Constitutional Court Joseph Kavarunganda, chief Arusha negotiator Boniface Ngulinzira, Parti Liberal leader Landwalkd Ndasingwa and his wife (who was Canadian). A few of those targeted through the list managed to survive, including the prime minister delegate Faustin Twagiramungu, but the assassination spree was generally very successful.

Dallaire was quoted as having said that the entirety of the moderate political leadership for Rwanda were all either in hiding or dead by noon, taking any hope for a moderate government in the future away from the people. Bagosora backed Augustin Bizimungu as his preferred candidate, but he was rejected by the crisis committee. This forced Bagosora to concede to Marcel Gatzinzi being appointed, who happened to be the only exception to Dallaire's assessment of all being lost. Gatzinzi did his best to negotiate for a ceasefire with the Rwandan Patriotic Front and tried to keep the national army from taking part in the genocide, but his tactics were seen as soft and he only lasted in office for ten days. At that point, the hardliner Bizimungu was put in office in his place.

The Rwandan Genocide

Within just a few hours of Habyarimana's death, the genocide itself officially began. The Rwandan Genocide refers to a massively large scale murder of Tutsi people on the basis of their ethnicity. The Gisenyl province was already the heartland of the akazu and it hosted Hutu military leaders that were the most organized participants in the beginning. The Interahamwe and Hutu civilians gathered so that the commanders could announce that the president was dead, putting the blame for the assassination on the shoulders of the Rwandan Patriotic Front. They proceeded to order the citizens to begin the mass murders, instructing them to spare no one and even kill the Tutsi babies.

From there, the murders spread to Kibuye, Ruhengeri, Kigali, Gikongoro, Cyangugu, and Kibungo on the 7th of April, Local officials were ordered by people in Kigali to spread false rumors that the Rwandan Patriotic Front was responsible for assassinating the president in every case and ordered civilians to carry out the plan to kill all Tutsi. The population of Hutu citizens were all used to being subservient to their government and it did not take very much to convince them to obey authority figures. They had also been given weapons during the previous months, and so they moved to carry out the order to murder without question.

Gitarama and Butare were two provinces that had a lower murder rate within the early phase of the genocide because the governors for both of these areas supported the moderates and did not agree with the violent plans. On April 9th, the genocide really began in Gitarama. In Butare, it began on the 19th of April, after the Tutsi governor by the name of Jean Baptiste Habyarimana was arrested and murdered. Any areas that were already being controlled by the Rwandan Patriotic Front were not affected by the genocide and remained unchanged, which included the easter Ruhengeri and parts of the Byumba province.

The gendarmerie, thePresidential Guard, and the youth militia combined their forces for the rest of April and the early part of May, killing the Tutsi very quickly with the help of local populations. It has been estimated that within the first six weeks there were Rwandan murders that numbered up to

800.000. The ultimate goal of this genocide was the literal definition of genocide: the total and complete eradication of the Tutsi that were living in Rwanda. The Rwandan Patriotic Front army was advancing, but it was the only opposing force that was there to slow and prevent these murders. Any domestic opposition had previously been eradicated, and UNAMIR operated under rules that expressly forbid it from using any force for anything but self-defense.

In the rural areas in Rwanda, it was easy for the Hutu to identify and kill their Tutsi neighbors, because they were all familiar with each other and well acquainted enough to have shared that information. Their families had all lived together, side by side, and they knew each other. In areas that were more urban, citizens could reside more anonymously to the public, so it was more difficult to find all of the Tutsi. In order to make the process of combing out the Tutsi easier, road blocks were erected, manned by the Interahame and military officials, and anyone that traveled passed the roadblock had to show their national identity card as a requirement. The identity cards contained information on ethnicity, and anyone carrying an identity card that labeled them as Tutsi was immediately slaughtered.

During the genocide, many Hutu were murdered as well. There were a variety of different reasons for the murder of fellow Hutu, which ranged from being a journalist and having an appearance that looked Tutsi to allegations that the Hutu victims were sympathizers for the moderate opposition parties and/or the Tutsi.

Slow and steady progress was being made by the Rwandan Patriotic Front in the north and eastern side of the country. As they made their gains, they ended the genocidal killings in each area that they began to occupy. The list of places that the Rwandan Patriotic Front had ended anti-Tutsi violence in by the end of April included Byumba, Kigali, Kibungo, and the Ruherengeri provinces. On the opposite end of the spectrum, the genocidal killings came to an end during April in Gisenyl, the heartlands of the akazu, because almost every single Tutsi life had been taken in that area. Once the Rwandan Patriotic Front conquered a new area, the Hutu population fled in large numbers because they were afraid that they would face similarly violent retribution for their part in the Tutsi genocide. For example, there were 500,000 residents of Kibungo that walked into Tanzania by route of the Bridge at Rusumo Falls, having walked on foot in the span of a few days. They were taken into camps run by the United Nations and effectively kept under control by Hutu regime leaders, all of which was done under the control of the former governor of Kibungo.

The genocidal killings of Tutsi continued through the months of May and June in the rest of the Rwandan provinces, although they had already lost their organization and had become sporadic and much lower-key. This was due to a combination of things, including the fact that the Tutsi had already been almost completely wiped out and the fact that the government wanted to calm the anarchy that had grown through these killings so that they could focus the population on fighting the Rwandan Patriotic Front instead.

A combined effort of the French-led mission of the United Nations called Operation Turquoise saw 2,500 soldiers enter the southwestern portion of Rwanda on the 23rd of June. The intentions of this mission were humanitarian in nature, but the soldiers involved were not able to save enough people for their presence to be considered significant. The authorities that participated in the genocide were incredibly quick to welcome the French and even donned the French flag on their vehicles to show how welcome they were, but would then turn instantly and slaughter any Tutsi who revealed themselves by coming out of hiding to look for protection.

The Rwandan Patriotic Front finally managed to complete their conquest of Rwanda in July, holding all of the country but the part that Operation Turquoise was already occupying. Kigali was taken by the Rwandan Patriotic Front on July 4th, with Gisenyl following with the rest of the northwest on July 18th. This marked the end of the genocide, A repeat of the results of the Rwandan Patriotic Front victory in Kibungo showed mass numbers of the Hutu population fleeing across the border. This time, the Hutu moved into Zaire, and they brought Bagosora and the other leaders of the government team that was behind the genocide with them.

Though most of the stories of the people that were involved in the Rwandan Genocide are dark because they are either the recipient of great violence or the cause of it, there were those that tried to do good as well. Several people are noted as having made attempts to shelter the mortally vulnerable Tutsi people or even stop their genocide completely. Romeo Dallaire was one of these people and a Canadian Lieutenant-General with UNAMIR, and so was the Ghanaian Deputy Commander of UNAMIR, Captain Mbaye Diagne was a Senegalese army officer that was also with UNAMIR and was responsible for saving many lives before he was killed. Henry Kwami Anyiodoho. Pierantonio Costa was an Italian diplomat that manages to rescue and save many lives. Another Italian volunteer by the name of Antonia Locatelli was murdered by members of the Interahamwe after she tried to save the lives of 300 to 400 Tutsi people by calling international community officials. A Hutu woman with the name of Jacqueline Mukansonera saved a Tutsi person during the period of genocide. A journalist and Hutu priest by the name of Andre Sibomana is also responsible for saving many lives. An Academy Award nominated film by the name of Hotel Rwanda was made about the man by the name of Paul Rusesabagina. Carl Wilkens is also noteworthy as the only American that decided to stay in Rwanda while the genocides were occurring.

The responsibility for the planning of the genocide of Tutsi people fell in the hands of the crisis committee, which took power in Rwanda immediately after the death of its former president, Habyarimana. They were the top authority in the nation and they planned and coordinated the genocide from start to finish. Bagosora wasted no time in throwing orders to kill all of the Tutsi, even speaking with groups from the Interahamwe in Kigali in person. He was also responsible for making phone calls to the leaders of other Rwandan provinces in order to spread the genocide and keep it going until all Tutsi were dead. Defense minister Augustin Bizimana was also one of the leading people that were responsible on a national level for the planning and organization of this genocide. Aloys Ntabakuze was responsible as the commander of the paratroopers. Protais Mpiranya was responsible as the head of the Presidential Guard. Felicien Kabuga was just a businessman, but he was responsible for funding the Interahamwe and the RTLM. Coordination of the Impuzamugami and Interahamwe militia activities across the nation were in the hands of Joseph Nzirorera and Pascal Musabe.

The planning and organization was led by the Presidential Guard in Kigali, where they were assisted by the Impuzamugambi and the Interahamwe. They were responsible for setting up the roadblocks that required every person passing them to show their identity cards, which labeled everyone by their ethnicity, allowing the Tutsi that revealed themselves at these stops to be taken to their immediate slaughter. The militias were also responsible for imposing searches through the houses within the city and murdering any Tutsi they could find, then looting their property afterward. Tharcisse Renzaho was the Kigali governor and he played a leading role as well and was even seen checking the roadblocks to make sure they were as effective as possible. He was also responsible for using his position of power to remove anyone from their own positions if they were not active enough in the killing of enough Tutsi.

The responsibility for organizing and overseeing the genocidal killings in rural areas was generally given to the local government hierarchy, allowing the rural areas to continue being responsible for their part in the killings in the same way that they were responsible for their other country duties. The emergency committee sent orders from Kigali, and the governor of every province would disseminate these instructions and give them to the district leaders, known as bourgmestres. These district leaders would then take give clear directions to all of the smaller leaders within the villages, cells, and sectors of their districts. Unlike genocides like the Holocaust, where soldiers are responsible for the majority of the death toll, the ordinary citizens of Rwanda are responsible for most of the murders, and that was especially true in rural areas. Because of the fact that the Hutu and Tutsi had lived side by side in these rural areas, the families knew each other well, so the Hutu among them already knew who was Tutsi and could target them immediately.

On April 8th, the crisis committee named Theodore Sindikubwabo their new interim president of Rwanda and Jaen Kambanda was given the title of new prime minister. They used the terms that are written in the 1991 constitution to make these designations, not the Arusha Accords. At that point, though all political parties did have some form of representation within the government, most of the officials involved were part of the Hutu Power movement or supported it. April 9th was the day that the interim government cabinet was sworn in, but they were immediately taken out of Kigali and moved to Gitarama to make sure that they were far enough away to avoid getting caught in the battles between the Rwandan Patriotic Front and the Rwandan army as they fought in the capital. At that time, there was no longer a need for the crisis committee, so it was dissolved in the official sense. However, Bagosora and the other senior officers that had been involved in the crisis committee continued to hold the position of de facto rulers. With this group at the forefront of the Hutu-run nation's government, they were able to mobilize the population of the nation, which makes them a legitimate regime, though it also effectively proved itself to be ineffective as well when it came time to halt the Interahamwe or the army's activities. Romeo Dallaire visited the headquarters of the Rwandan government only a full week after it had been formed and he reported seeing most of the government spending time in leisure. According to Dallaire, the most strenuous of activities was still nothing more than busywork that would do nothing for the nation in the near future or anytime soon.

The means behind these killings and the events that led to making this genocide possible are rather complex, and some of them rely on the human psychology that explains how the past makes victims of abuse or political domination respond to authority later on in life. For the government, the ability to follow through with their plans for the total annihilation of the Tutsi people was with a perfectly harmonized combination of efforts between a variety of the resources that they had at hand. One of those resources was the people, and for the Hutu people of Rwanda, the ability to follow through with the orders to brutally murder their Tutsi neighbors came from another combination of efforts that were just as perfectly harmonized. The groundwork for these orders making sense and being carried out was a systematic education of the Hutu population through propaganda and the harsh truths of history that told all Hutu citizens that they could not trust their Tutsi neighbors and that they should consider them all to be dangerous enemies. The truths in history that taught them that the Tutsi could do them wrong came in painful memories that mirrored the different forms of slavery found in other countries. Tutsi had been treated as racially superior by other groups of people, and the Tutsi regarded themselves as better as well. They had more social privilege, they were given all of the better jobs, they were put in charge of everything important, and they were more well off financially. Part of this privilege was command and control of the Hutu, which was often used in ways that forced the Hutu into servitude and submission. This learned submission would forever teach those that had lived through those hardships to think obediently when ordered by their government. The third and final factor was duress, which reminded the Hutu people that if they chose to not obey, they would be slandered as Tutsi sympathizers and that would lead to their own deaths as well. In essence, it was kill or be killed.

Observers from the United Nations watched on April 9th as a polish church in Gikondo was attacked and children were massacred. 1,000 European troops that were heavily trained and heavily armed showed up on the same day to take European civilian personnel to safety outside of the country. The troops did leave, despite the anarchy in the country around them, and they did not help UNAMIR efforts. The media began covering the events on the 9th as well, starting with a report by the Washington Post on an incident where Rwandan employees that worked for a relief agency were killed while their expatriate colleagues watched.

Another case of Tutsi massacre during the period of genocide took place on April 11th. Thousands of Tutsi refugees had taken up residence within the Official Technical School in Kigali, made safer by the presence of Belgian soldiers with UNAMIR. When the soldiers withdrew on April 11th, the armed forces of Rwanda and militia members took advantage and massacred all of the Tutsi.

Another massacre like the one that was shared with the world on April 9th happened three days later in the same month, on April 12th. Hidden in a Catholic church in Nyange, and then in a Kivumu commune, a group of over 1,500 Tutsi people were looking to find refuge. The local authorities worked with the local members of the Interahamwe to coordinate the use of bulldozers to knock down the whole church building with all of the Tutsi still inside of it. Every single person that tried to escape from death in the church while it was being demolished were killed by the machetes and rifles of the militia instead. The local priest that was responsible for the church was later convicted of both crimes against humanity and the crime of genocide for his part in its demolition.

In all of the killings brought on by the genocide, the large majority of them were killed in their own towns or villages, and they were most often killed by their neighbors and people they were aware of or knew personally before the genocide. There were orders given through both local and government-sponsored programs on the radio that demanded the killings of all Tutsi people by the Hutu population. Those that were not persuaded by the orders were killed on the spot.

The exception to all of the local violence was found in the Butare Province, where Jean-Baptiste Habyarimana remained the only prefect of Tutsi descent and he governed over the only province that was dominated by a party in support of the opposition. Habyarimana did not agree with the genocide, and he opposed it within his province and was able to keep the citizens relatively calm all the way up until the extremist Sylvain Ndikumana deposed him. Even after Habyarimana was deposed and their new leader began ordering them to follow the rest of the country into genocidal killings, the public resisted the idea of murdering people that they knew, so the government brought members of their militia in from Kigali on a helicopter. The militia had no problem following the orders to murder the Tutsi in their stead.

The main weapon used by militia members was the machete, and some were given rifles as well. The Hutu gangs were known for hunting and massacring victims that were hiding out and trying to stay safe in school buildings and churches.

One of the biggest weapons of the Interahamwe, who were the biggest perpetrators, was rape. They used it in order to further dehumanize the Tutsi population in the eyes of the Hutu citizens, and they used it in order to demoralize and dramatically exhaust the Tutsi. In order to be able to get the Hutu people to use rape as a weapon, propaganda was an important tool. The government was able to use it in order to instill both the racial hate required to fuel the genocide as well as a very gender specific form of violence. Within the propaganda distributed by the Hutu government, the Tutsi women were all sexually seductive and in league with the enemies of the Hutu.

The fact that the enactments of these rapes were so violent, and the fact that Hutu women were complicated and also participated in them, suggests that the propaganda had the desired effect on the mind of Hutu society. Soldiers in the Army for the Liberation of Rwanda, soldiers in the Rwandan Defence Forces (including members of the Presidential Guard), and civilians were all urged to commit rapes that were mostly targeted against Tutsi women. The Tutsi were always the main targets in any scenario involved in this genocide, but moderate Tutsi women were also raped. Hutu women that hid Tutsis or were married to a Tutsi were also targeted for rape. With the use of the propaganda, force, and threats, anyone in the area while a rape was going on was forced to stand by and do nothing. Testimonials from women during the genocide period mention being raped as many as five times a day and having to see people watching without stepping forward to help. They were also treated with no pity afterward, and were forced to continue to farm and work for the Hutu in between being raped.

HIV and AIDS was also a big part of the rape initiative. On top of demoralizing the victim, those that became infected with HIV or AIDS would then have to face a future that held their slow and painful death from an incurable disease. While the conflict in Rwanda flared, Hutu extremists moved from hospital to hospital, releasing patients that were infected with AIDS so that they could form rape squads that were made up of hundreds of HIV and AIDS infected people that were then set out into Rwanda to rape as many Tutsi women as they could find.

Another intention behind the rapes was the intention of ruining the Tutsi women's ability to have children. It was not uncommon for sexual mutilation to happen after a rape, with some of the common means of doing so including mutilation of the vagina with knives, machetes, boiling water, acid, and sharpened sticks.

Experts have estimated that somewhere in between 250,000 and 500,000 women suffered through brutal rape during the genocide of the Tutsi people.

The sexual violence was mainly pointed at the women, but there were instances of sexual violence against men as well. They were very seldom the victims of war rape, but they did suffer through genital mutilations, which included cutting them off completely and displaying them in public as trophies.

The other of the three original occupants of Rwanda, the Twa, were pygmy people that were now sometimes called the Batwa. During the months that prepared the nation for the genocide, the Hutu radio stations started accusing the Batwa of supporting and helping the Rwandan Patriotic Front. At the time of the genocide, their numbers made up somewhere around 1% of the population of Rwanda at 30,000. By the end of the genocide, that number was staggeringly cut down to 20,000. Sometimes, the Two are called the forgotten victims of the Rwandan Genocide. The members of the Twa that survived the genocide have stated that the Hutu fighters had threatened to kill them all.

Because of the fact that everything in Rwanda was so chaotic at the time, it is unknown exactly how many people were killed during the genocide. In the instance of the Khmer Rouge in Cambodia or Nazi Germany, efforts were made by the governments to record the number of people that were killed. That did not happen in Rwanda, there were no attempts made by any authorities to make any kind of effort towards counting the dead, only making them dead. The members of the Rwandan Patriotic Front that found themselves in government positions after the genocide made an official statement with the number 1,071,000 as their estimation for the number killed. 10% of that approximation represented Hutu deaths. There are those that agree that an estimate of one million is plausible, while others (like the UN) think that the death toll is probably closer to 800,000. Other groups establish the number approximately 750,000. Aegis Trust author, James Smith was quoted saying, "What's important to remember is that there was a genocide. There was an attempt to eliminate Tutsis- men, women, and children- and to erase any memory of their existence."

84% of the 7.3 million people in Rwanda were Hutu, 15% of them were Tutsi, and 1% Twa. Out of that 7.3 million population figure before the genocide, 1,070,014 people were killed during the 100 days of genocide, according to the official reports from the Rwandan government. In total, the estimated number of surviving Tutsi is estimated to be around 300,000. Thousands of women were made to become widows, and many of the women in general had been raped multiple times and had since contracted HIV or AIDS. The children were affected too, with there being somewhere around 400,000 newly orphaned children, with around 85,000 of them having to become the leader in their home because there was nobody else to do it.

The Aftermath

After the Rwanda Patriotic Front finally reached victory, there were about two million Hutu people that immediately fled into neighboring countries to inhabit refugee camps. The Hutu people were afraid that they would be forced to face some form of revenge against them for the acts they committed against the Tutsi people during the genocide. One of the main Hutu attractors was Zaire. One of the problems with the refugee camps was that they were so full of people that were trying to live in cramped space, leaving them overcrowded. The overcrowding made it easier for the disease to spread. Epidemics took the lives of thousands of Hutu refugees that died of things like dysentery and cholera.

Though these refugee camps were officially organized by people with the United Nations High Commissioner for Refugees, it would be more realistic to say that they were run by the former Hutu regime with the backing of their army. Many of the leading people involved in the genocide were part of this refugee power, and they began preparing for their return to Rwanda.

The genocide had the unintended consequence of drastically changing the economy and the situation around the resources that Rwanda had to bring it back to life. Many of the buildings that had formerly given something back to the community by serving a purpose were now completely uninhabitable. When the former regime, run by Hutu leadership, had fled the country at the end of the genocide, they had taken all of the country's currency and monetary assets with them. The population was drastically lower, after 40% of the population was killed or had fled due to the violence of the genocide. Most of the people that were left were traumatized by the events they had witnessed and endured; most people had lost loved ones and relatives during the genocide, many had been the witness to murders and rapes, while even more had participated in the atrocities committed during the genocide. Many of the citizens were focused on the long-term effects of the use of rape as weapon during war, which included sexually transmitted diseases, social isolation, and unwanted pregnancies and babies. Some women were so desperate that they even forced themselves to suffer through abortions that they enacted upon themselves.

Though organizations that were not related to the government started to move back into Rwanda after the genocide was over and a semblance of peace returned, there was no significant amount of assistance given by the international community to the new regime. Most of the international assistance that came into that region was given to the refugee camps to host the Hutu that had liquidated from Rwanda and headed for Zaire.

Domestically, Kagame was determined to make sure that the government portrayed itself as inclusive, not just a Tutsi dominated force. He wanted to be clear that his place in office was not meant to force the Hutu to be subservient or to put the Tutsi in power. He ordered and organized an edit to their identity cards that removed the spot on it that distinguished a person's ethnicity. There was even a policy that was enacted while he was in office that began to lower the importance of the distinctions between the Twa, the Hutu, and the Tutsi people.

By the later part of the year 1996, there were Hutu militants that came from the refugee camps that were then launching cross-border missions into Rwanda on a regular basis. The Rwandan Patriotic Front was still in control of the government and used their position to fight back by launching a counteroffensive. Troops and military training were provided to the Zairian South Kivu province that was run by a Tutsi group called the Banyamulenge. This assistance allowed to reach their own victory and then the Banyamulenge joined the Rwandan forces and other Sairaian Tutsi in attacking refugee camps. The purpose was to target and destroy the Hutu militia so that they could no longer pose a threat to any group of inhabitants within Rwanda. During these attacks, hundreds of thousands of refugees were forced to flee. Many of them even made their way back into Rwanda, even though they knew that the Rwandan Patriotic Front still held a strong presence and control there. Others fled further west and made their way into Zaire.

Though they had scattered greatly and their numbers were much smaller than they had been before, the members of the former Hutu leadership continued to send insurgents across the border into Rwanda. In the beginning of these missions, they had the support of the native population and could move safely without caution. By the year 1999, the Tutsi-run government changed that by running their own series of propaganda and they started allowing Hutu citizens to join the national army. A combination of these two things gave the Rwandan Patriotic Front what it needed to finally pull the Hutu citizens back towards their side, which allowed them to defeat the insurgence.

On top of scattering the population of refugee Hutu and dismantling the refugee camps, Kagame also had his eyes set on a war that he had been planning with the intention of taking the president and long-time dictator Mobutu Sese Seko out of power. The genocidaires had found support in Mobutu previously, and he was also accused of personally allowing Tutsi people to be attacked within Zaire.

The Rwandan government paired with Uganda in support of an alliance between the four rebel groups. This was the beginning of the First Congo War, which began in 1996. The rebel alliance seized the control of the South and North Kivu provinces quickly and then later moved west, adding territory to their name by taking it from the demotivated and poorly organized Zairian army after just a small time spent fighting. They controlled the whole country by 1997 and Mobutu was forced to flee in exile. Zaire was then renamed the Democratic Republic of the Congo.

Peace did not last long, and the government in Rwanda stopped getting along with the new government in the Congo in 1998. Kagame was quick to support the idea of another new rebellion, which lead to the Second Congo War. This war was the cause of millions of deaths, a massive amount of damage, and continued to last until 2003. In 2010, the United Nations released a report that pointed a finger at the Rwandan army, accusing them of committing the crimes of large scale violations of human rights as well as crimes against humanity during those wars in the Congo. However, all charges and allegations have been denied by the government of Rwanda.

Moving back to the genocide and the months directly after the victory of the Rwandan Patriotic Front, there were many people that the Rwanda Patriotic Front killed because they were accused of supporting or participating in the genocide. Many of the Rwandan Patriotic Front soldiers that participated in these killings of genocide perpetrators and supporters were new recruits that had lost the lives of family and friends and wanted to taste revenge.

Many of the details of the Rwandan Genocide are disputed, including the scope, the scale, and where the responsibility belongs if it is going to be ultimately handed to one person or group of persons. Scholars and members of the Human Rights Watch have claimed numbers as high as 100,000 after the genocide. Some people even claim that the elite members of the Rwandan Patriotic Force and Kagame himself were tolerated the fact that people were being killed or were behind the organization of them. Kagame did acknowledge these killings of genocide perpetrators and supporters in an interview with journalist Stephen Kinzer, but he also said that the people responsible for organizing these killings were rogue soldiers that were impossible for him to control. In 1995, these killings that were potentially being carried out by the Rwandan Patriotic Front were given attention internationally after the Kibeho massacre. During this event, soldiers were seen opening fire on a camp in Butare Province filled with internally displaced people. An internally displaced person is an individual that has had to flee their home because of force but it still living somewhere within the borders of their own home country. Legally, they are not refugees, but they are often referred to as them. There were Australian soldiers that watched as they were serving with the UNAMIR that calculated the death toll to be at least 4,000 people dead. However, the Rwandan government's claim that was later made was a total 338 deaths.

One major problem that came to light during the civil war in Rwanda and the genocide was the judicial system being systematically destroyed. After the genocide was over and it came time to dole out punishments to those that were to blame for the deaths of so many innocent people, it became clear that as many as one million people had the potential of being culpable for some heinous crime associated with the genocide. That meant that almost a full one fifth of the population was potentially guilty of a terrible crime and was in need of being pushed through the court systems and then dealt with accordingly. To solve this problem, the Rwandan Patriotic Front arrested people en masse for their roles in the genocide, pursuing and jailing a total of over 100,000 people during the two years following the genocide. The Rwandan prison system was physically overwhelmed by the number of people it so suddenly had to house. This overcrowding problem led to conditions that were deemed inhuman, cruel, or degrading treatment by Amnesty International. The maximum capacity given to the nineteen prisons in Rwanda in their design plans was a total of about eighteen thousand inmates. At their peak in 1998, there was a total of 100,000 people being held in the detention facilities located across the nation.

The problem that was faced after finding the people who may be legally responsible for their parts in the genocide was the fact that the institutions within the government had been destroyed. That included the judicial courts, and to top things off, a good number of the prosecutors, judges, and employees of the legal system had been murdered. There were 750 judges in total before the genocide. 506 of them could no longer be found after it. Many of them were murdered while others fled the country. There were only an approximated fifty lawyers inside of Rwanda by 1997. Because of these difficult obstacles, the judicial system in Rwanda was incredibly slow. That meant that the court proceedings meant to find and prosecute those that were responsible for the Rwandan Genocide were slow. By the time trials began, there were 130,000 people that were suspected of having legal responsibility being held and awaiting trial. Between the four year span between 1996 and 2000, a total of 3,343 cases were completed. 20% of the defendants in those four years were given death sentences, 32% were given sentences of life in prison, and 20% were lucky enough to be acquitted of all charges. At the speed that they were going, experts estimated that it would take more than 200 years for them to put all of the suspected people in the prisons through proper trials. That time estimate did not include the trials of the suspects that were still at large.

The Organic Law was an official legal action that made the prosecution of crimes that were committed during the genocide as well as any crimes against humanity that was committed after October of 1990. With this law, the domestic courts were established as the core mechanism for responding to cases that were linked to the genocide. The law was amended in 2001, with the addition of the Gacaca courts as a second mechanism of response. In the Organic Law, there are four categories that are established to organize those that were involved in the genocide. These categories specify how far punishments for each type of offender are allowed to go. In the first category of this law, the people that were involved in organizing, planning, supervising, leading, or instigating the genocide are partnered with anyone who used their positions within the state's authority to support the genocide.

Those that did not belong to any of the previously mentioned groups, but established themselves as top offenders through their unique cruelty or an apparent enjoyment of the genocide, were also put into this group, as well as anyone that took part in sexual torture. If a person was in this group, a death sentence could be in their future.

It might be interesting to know that Rwanda had the death penalty within their judicial system before the Organic Law was born in 1996, but they hadn't actually executed anyone since 1982. In April of 1997, a total of twenty-two people broke that record when they were publically executed via firing squad. There were no more executions after the one event, though the Rwandan court system did continue to hand out death sentenced in regards to the Rwandan Genocide until 2003. The death penalty itself, perhaps inspired by the violence in Rwanda's history, was abolished on July 25th in 2007. With this action, anyone who had been looking at the death penalty saw their sentences changed to life in prison under solitary confinement.

The amended to the Organic Law in 2001 that added the Gacaca courts into their response team for the trials against those suspected of crimes during the genocide came into being based solely on the vast number of people that were the court system needed to put on trial and either release from jail or cement their punishment in the name of justice. The more severe cases were still taken by the local government and handled by those with whom it most concerned, but the Gacaca were given some of the less severe cases to bring to trial.

The objectives of the Gacaca courts included:

- Finding the truth about what exactly happened during the genocide
- Making the process of the genocide trials go faster
- Fighting lawfully against the culture of impunity
- Adding to the sense of national unity and helping with the process of reconciliation
- Proving that the Rwandan people are capable of solving their own problem

Traditionally, the Gacaca court system was meant to deal with the conflicts that arose within communities as a sort of small time, domestic court. The function was modified and the court system was adapted so that it would be able to handle the bigger problems of genocidal crimes. There were a series of different modifications to the Gacaca court systems that were made in order to enhance the functionality. At this time, the estimated number of cases that the Gacaca court system has put through trials is over on million.

As their contribution to furthering the humanity in society, the United Nations created a group called the International Criminal Tribunal for Rwanda, which is based in Arusha in Tanzania at this time. The Tribunal that was created by the United Nations has legal jurisdiction and oversees those that sit in high-level positions within the armed forces and the government. Rwanda is still responsible for the prosecution of local people and the lower-level leaders, but the United Nation's Tribunal has jurisdiction of the higher-level members of people who sit in Rwandan government and within the higher-level ranks of their armed forces.

Printed in Great Britain
by Amazon

38133084R00057